Duncles 50 Grea

GW00402447

Photographs from the Father Francis Brown (1880-1960) collection
have been used with the kind permission of the administrators.
Cover photo by Brian Lynch: - Traditional Music, Culturlann,
Monkstown, Co. Dublin. Courtesy of Bord Fáilte.

Layout, Design and Typesetting by Grace O'Halloran.
Cover by Niche Design, Dublin.

Printed by Watermans, Cork.

Nancy Spain Copyright Control
The Rare Oul' Times ©Pete St. John
Working Man Copyright Control

Ossian Publications Ltd., P.O. Box 84, Cork, Ireland

OMB 82

ISBN 0 946 005 63 X

SPANCIL HILL

Em   D
Last night as I lay dreaming
         Em
Of pleasant days gone by,

Me mind bein' bent on rambling
  G   D
To Ireland I did fly,
  Em
I stepped aboard a vision
     G   D
And followed with my will,
  Em   D
Till next I came to anchor
          Em
At the cross near Spancil Hill.

Delighted by the novelty,
Enchanted with the scene,
Where in my early boyhood
Where often I had been.
I thought I heard a murmur
And I think I hear it still,
It's the little stream of water
That flows down Spancil Hill.

It being the twenty-third of June,
The day before the fair,
When Ireland's sons and daughters
In crowds assembled there.
The young, the old, the brave and the bold,
They came for sport and kill,
There were jovial conversations
At the cross of Spancil Hill.

I went to see my neighbours,
To hear what they might say,
The old ones were all dead and gone,
The others turning grey.
I met with tailor Quigley,
He's as bold as ever still,
Sure he used to make my britches
When I lived in Spancil Hill.

I paid a flying visit
To my first and only love,
She's white as any lily
And gentle as a dove.
She threw her arms around me,
Saying 'Johnny, I love you still'
She's Mag, the farmer's daughter
And the pride of Spancil Hill.

I dreamt I stooped and kissed her
As in the days of yore,
She said 'Johnny, you're only joking,
As many's the time before.'
The cock crew in the morning,
He crew both loud and shrill,
And I woke in California,
Many miles from Spancil Hill.

ROSIN THE BOW

G
I've travelled all over this world,
                   C
And now to another I'll go,
  G   C
And I know that good quarters are waiting,
G   D   G
To welcome old Rosin the Bow.

CHORUS:
G   C
To welcome old Rosin the Bow,
  G   C
To welcome old Rosin the Bow,
   G   C
And I know that good quarters are waiting,
  G   D   G
To welcome old Rosin the Bow.

When I'm dead and laid out on the counter
A voice you will hear from below,
Saying, 'Send down a hogshead of whiskey
To drink with old Rosin the Bow'.

And get half a dozen stout fellows,
And stack 'em up in a row,
Let them drink out of half gallon bottles
to the memory of Rosin the Bow.
REPEAT CHORUS

Get this half dozen stout fellows,
And let them all stagger and go,
And dig a great hole in the meadow
And in it put Rosin the Bow.

Get ye a couple of bottles,
Put one at my head and me toe,
With a diamond ring scratch upon them
The name of old Rosin the Bow.
REPEAT CHORUS

I feel that old tyrant approaching,
That cruel remorseless old foe,
And I lift up me glass in his honour,
Take a drink with old Rosin the Bow.

MONTO

```
G                C
Well, if you've got a wing-o,
G              C
Take her up to Ring-o,
G                 C
Where the waxies sing-o,
D     G
All the day.
```

```
                         C
If you've had your fill of porter
        G          C
And you can't go any further,
G            C
Give your man the order:
D        G
Back to the Quay!
```

CHORUS:

```
                  C     G      C
And take her up to Monto, Monto, Monto,
G           C        D   G   D G
Take her up to Monto, langeroo - To you!
```

You've heard of the Duke of Gloucester,
The dirty old imposter,
He got a mot and lost her,
Up the Furry Glen,
He first put on his bowler
And he buttoned up his trousers,
And he whistled for a growler
And he says, 'My man'
Take me up to   etc.

You've heard of the Dublin Fusileers,
The dirty old bamboozileers,
They went and got the childer,
One, two, three.
Oh, marching from the Linen Hall,
There's one for every cannonball,
And Vick's going to send them all,
O'er the sea.
But first go up to   etc.

When Carey told on Skin-the-goat,
O'Donnell caught him on the boat,
He wished he'd never been afloat,
The filthy skite,
It wasn't very sensible
To tell on the Invincibles,
They stood up for their principles,
Day and night.
And they all went up to   etc.

Now when the Czar of Russia
And the King of Prussia,
Landed in the Phoenix Park
In a big balloon,
They asked the polismen to play
'The wearing of the green'
But the buggers in the depot
Didn't know the tune.
So they both went up to   etc.

Now the Queen she came to call on us,
She wanted to see all of us,
I'm glad she didn't fall on us,
She's eighteen stone.
'Mister Melord the Mayor', says she,
'Is this all you've got to show me?'
'Why, no ma'am, there's some more to see,
Póg mo thóin'
And he took her up to   etc.

Pointsman at Nassau Street, Dublin, 1939

THE JUICE OF THE BARLEY

D
In the sweet County Limerick
   G   A
One cold winter's night,
     D
All the turf fires were burning
   A
When I first saw the light.
     D   G
And a drunken old midwife
     D
Went tipsy with joy,

As she danced round the floor
     G   A
With her slip of a boy.

CHORUS:
            D   G D
Singing bainne na mbo is a gamhna
          A   D
And the juice of the barley for me.

Well when I was a gossoon
Of eight year or so,
With me turf and me primer
To school I did go,
To a dusty old schoolhouse
Without any door,
Where lay the schoolmaster
Blind drunk on the floor.
REPEAT CHORUS

At the learning I wasn't
Such a genius I'm thinking,
But I soon bet the master
Entirely at drinking,
Not a wake or a wedding
For five miles around,
But meself in the corner
Was sure to be found.
REPEAT CHORUS

One day the priest
Read me out from the altar,
Saying you'll end up your days
With your neck in a halter,
And you'll dance a fine jig
Between heaven and hell,
And his words they did frighten
The truth for to tell.
REPEAT CHORUS

So the very next morning
As the dawn it did break,
I went down to the vestry
The pledge for to take,
And there in that room
Sat the priests in a bunch,
Round a big roaring fire
Drinking tumblers of punch.
REPEAT CHORUS

Well from that day to this
I have wandered alone,
I'm a jack of all trades
And a master of none,
With the sky for me roof
And the earth for me floor,
And I'll dance out me days
Drinking whiskey galore.
REPEAT CHORUS

THE BOG DOWN
IN THE VALLEY-O

CHORUS:
G   C
O-ro the rattlin' bog,
     G   D
the bog down in the valley-o
G   C
O-ro the rattlin' bog,
     G   D   G
the bog down in the valley-o.

1.
And in that bog there was a tree,
a rare tree, a rattlin' tree,
with a tree in the bog
and the bog down in the valley-o.
REPEAT CHORUS
2.
Now on that tree there was a limb
3.
Now on that limb there was a branch
4.
Now on that branch there was a twig
5.
Now on that twig there was a nest
6.
Now in that nest there was an egg
7.
Now in that egg there was a bird
8.
Now on that bird there was a feather
9.
Now on that feather there was a flea

DEAR OLD IRELAND

```
G                                        D         G
Deep in Canadian woods we've met, from one bright island flown,
                                     D              G
Great is the land we tread, but yet our hearts are with our own.
    Am              C              G              D
And ere we leave this shanty small, while fades the autumn day,
    G                         D              G
We'll toast old Ireland, dear old Ireland, Ireland boys Hurrah!
```

CHORUS:
```
D              C    G              D
Ireland boys Hurrah, oh Ireland boys Hurrah,
    G                         D              G
We'll toast old Ireland, dear old Ireland, Ireland boys Hurrah!
```

We've heard her faults a hundred times, the new ones and the old,
In songs and sermons, rants and rhymes, enlarged some fifty-fold.
But take them all, the great and small, and this we've got to say:
Here's dear old Ireland! Good old Ireland! Ireland boys Hurrah!

We know that brave and good men tried, to snap her rusty chain,
The patriots suffered, martyrs died, and all 'tis said, in vain:
But no boy, no! a glance will show, how far they've won their way -
Here's good old Ireland! Loved old Ireland! Ireland boys Hurrah!

We've seen the wedding and the wake, the patron and the fair;
And lithe young frames at the dear old games, in the kindly Irish air.
And the loud 'Hurroo', we have heard it too, and a thundering 'clear the way!'
Here's gay old Ireland! Dear old Ireland! Ireland boys Hurrah!

And well we know in cool grey eyes, when the hard day's work is o'er,
How soft and sweet are the words that greet, the friends who meet once more.
With 'Mary Machree!' and 'My Pat, 'tis he!' and 'my own heart night and day!'
Ah, fond old Ireland! Dear old Ireland! Ireland boys Hurrah!

And happy and bright are the groups that pass, from their peaceful homes, for miles,
O'er fields and roads, and hills, to Mass, when Sunday morning smiles!
And deep the zeal their true hearts feel, when low they kneel and pray,
O, dear old Ireland! Blest old Ireland! Ireland boys Hurrah!

But deep in Canadian woods, we've met, and we never may see again,
The dear old isle where our hearts are set, and our first fond hopes remain!
But come, fill up another cup, and with every sup let's say:
'Here's loved old Ireland! Good old Ireland! Ireland boys Hurrah!'

The School Bus, Crossmolina, Co. Mayo, 1938

THE MERMAID

G   C   C   C   D   G
It was Friday morn when we set sail and we were not far from the land.
                      C   G   C   D   G
When our captain he spied a mermaid so fair, with a comb and a glass in her hand.

CHORUS:
          C   G   D
And the ocean waves do roll and the stormy winds do blow
G   C   G
And we poor sailors are skipping at the top
       C   D   G
While the landlubbers lie down below, below, below,
       C   D   G
While the landlubbers lie down below.

Then up spoke the captain of our gallant ship, and a fine old man was he.
'This fishy mermaid has warned me of our doom, we shall sink to the bottom of the sea.'
REPEAT CHORUS

Then up spoke the mate of our gallant ship, and a fine spoken man was he.
Saying 'I have a wife in Brooklyn by the sea, and tonight a widow she will be.'
REPEAT CHORUS

Then up spoke the cabin boy of our gallant ship, and a brave young lad was he.
'Oh I have a sweetheart in Salem by the sea, and tonight she'll be weeping for me.'
REPEAT CHORUS

Then up spoke the cook of our gallant ship, and a crazy old butcher was he.
'I care much more for my pots and my pans than I do for the bottom of the sea.'
REPEAT CHORUS

Then three times 'round spun our gallant ship, and three times 'round spun she.
Three times 'round spun our gallant ship, and she sank to the bottom of the sea.
REPEAT CHORUS

THE WILD COLONIAL BOY

D   Em
There was a wild colonial boy,
   A   D
Jack Duggan was his name,
             A
He was born and raised in Ireland
         D
In a place called Castlemain,
           A
He was his father's only son,
G   A   D
His mother's pride and joy,
             Em
And dearly did his parents love
   A   D
The Wild Colonial Boy.

At the early age of sixteen years
He left his native home,
And through Australia's sunny clime
He was inclined to roam.
He robbed the lordly squatters,
Their flocks he would destroy,
A terror to Australia
Was the Wild Colonial Boy.

For two long years this daring youth
Ran on his wild career,
With a heart that knew no danger,
Their justice did not fear.
He stuck the Beechworth coach up,
And he robbed Judge McEvoy,
Who, trembling, gave his gold up
To the Wild Colonial Boy.

He bade the judge 'Good morning'
And he told him to beware,
For he never robbed an honest judge
What acted 'on the square'.
'Yet you would rob a mother
Of her son and only joy,
And breed a race of outlaws
Like the Wild Colonial Boy.'

One morning on the prairie
Wild Jack Duggan rode along,
While listening to the mocking birds
Singing a cheerful song.
Out jumped three troopers fierce and grim,
Kelly, Davis and FitzRoy,
They all set out to capture him,
The Wild Colonial Boy.

'Surrender now, Jack Duggan,
You can see there's three to one,
Surrender in the Queen's name, sir,
You are a plundering son.'
Jack drew two pistols from his side
And glared upon FitzRoy,
'I'll fight, but not surrender',
Cried the Wild Colonial Boy.

He fired point blank at Kelly
And brought him to the ground.
He fired a shot at Davis, too
Who fell dead at the sound,
But a bullet pierced his brave young heart
From the pistol of FitzRoy,
And that was how they captured him -
The Wild Colonial Boy.

CARRICKFERGUS

D   Em   A   D
I wish I was in Carrickfergus,
        Em   A   D
Only for nights in Ballygrant,
             A   D
I would swim over the deepest ocean,
        Em   A   D
Only for nights in Ballygrant.

                                   A
But the sea is wide and I can't swim over,
     D   A
Nor have I the wings to fly.
G   A   D
If I could find me a handsome boatsman,
          Em A   D
To ferry me over to my love and die.

Now in Kilkenny,
It is reported,
They've marble stones
As black as ink,
With gold and silver
I would transport her,
But I'll sing no more now
'Till I get a drink.
I'm drunk today,
But then I'm seldom sober,
A handsome rover from town to town.
Ah, but I'm sick now,
My days are over,
Come all ye young lads
And lay me down.

PADDY WORKS ON THE RAILWAY

D   A
In eighteen hundred and forty-one, my corduroy breeches I put on,
D   A   D A
My corduroy breeches I put on, to work upon the railway.

CHORUS:
                         D   G D   A   D
The railway, I'm weary of the railway, poor Paddy works on the railway.

In eighteen hundred and forty two, I didn't know what I should do,
I didn't know what I should do, to work upon the railway.
REPEAT CHORUS

In eighteen hundred and forty three, I took a trip across the sea,
I took a trip across the sea, to work upon the railway.
REPEAT CHORUS

In eighteen hundred and forty four, I landed on Columbia's shore,
I landed on Columbia's shore, to work upon the railway.
REPEAT CHORUS

In eighteen hundred and forty five, when Daniel O'Connell was alive,
When Daniel O'Connell was alive, to work upon the railway.
REPEAT CHORUS

In eighteen hundred and forty six, I changed my trade to carrying bricks,
I changed my trade to carrying bricks, to work upon the railway.
REPEAT CHORUS

In eighteen hundred and forty seven, poor Paddy was thinking of going to heaven,
Poor Paddy was thinking of going to heaven, to work upon the railway.
REPEAT CHORUS

In eighteen hundred and forty eight,I learned to take my whiskey straight,
I learned to take my whiskey straight, to work upon the railway.
REPEAT CHORUS

THE NIGHTINGALE

D
As I went a-walking
    A   D
One morning in May,

I met a young couple
           A
Who fondly did stray,
   D
And one was a young maid
        A
So sweet and so fair,
       D   G
And the other was a soldier
      D
And a brave grenadier.

CHORUS:
D   G
And they kissed so sweet and comforting
     D
As they clung to each other,

They went arm in arm along the road
         A
Like sister and brother,
      D
They went arm in arm along the road
       A
Till they came to a stream,
       D   G
And they both sat down together
       D
To hear the nightingale sing.

From out of his knapsack
He took a fine fiddle,
And he played her such merry tunes
As you ever did hear,
And he played her such merry tunes
That the valley did ring,
And they both sat down together
To hear the nightingale sing.
REPEAT CHORUS

O soldier, o soldier
Will you marry me
O no said the soldier,
That never can be
For I have my own wife at home
In my own counteree
And she is the sweetest little thing
That you ever did see.
REPEAT CHORUS

Now I'm off to India
For seven long years,
Drinking wines and strong whiskey
Instead of cool beers;
And if I ever return again
It'll be in the spring,
And we'll both sit down together
And hear the nightingale sing.
REPEAT CHORUS

WILL YOU GO,
LASSIE, GO?

G
Oh, the summertime is coming
       C   G
And the trees are sweetly blooming
       C   G   Em
And the wild mountain thyme
      Am   C
Grows around the blooming heather,
  G C   G
Will ye go, lassie, go?

CHORUS:
          C   G
And we'll all go together
        C   G   Em
To pluck wild mountain thyme,
       C
All around the blooming heather,
  G C   G
Will ye go, lassie, go?

I will build my love a tower
Near yon pure crystal fountain,
And on it I will pile
All the flowers of the mountain,
Will ye go, lassie, go?
REPEAT CHORUS

If my true love she were gone,
I would surely find another,
Where wild mountain thyme
Grows around the blooming heather,
Will ye go, lassie, go?
REPEAT CHORUS

12

Carrying the turf, Belmullet, Co. Mayo, 1935

THE FOGGY DEW

```
Am                    G
As down the glen one Easter morn
   C   Am
To a city fair rode I,
                 G
There armed lines of marching men
   C        Am
In squadrons passed me by.
   C          G      C
No pipe did hum, no battle drum
                    Am
Did sound its dread tattoo,
                         G
But the Angelus bell o'er the Liffey swell,
   C              Am
Rang out through the Foggy Dew.
```

'Twas England bade our Wild Geese 'Go',
That small nations might be free
But their lonely graves are by Suvla's waves
Or the fringe of the great North Sea.
Oh, had they died by Pearse's side,
Or fought with Cathal Brugha,
Their names we'd keep where the Fenians sleep,
'Neath the shroud of the Foggy Dew.

Right proudly high over Dublin town
They hung out the flag of war.
'Twas better to die 'neath an Irish sky
Than at Suvla or Sud el Bar;
And from the plains of Royal Meath
Strong men came hurrying through,
While Brittania's Huns, with their great big guns,
Sailed in through the Foggy Dew.

But the bravest fell and the requiem bell
Rang mournfully and clear,
For those who died that Easter tide,
In the springtime of the year;
While the world did gaze with deep amaze,
At those fearless men but few,
Who bore the fight, that freedom's light
Might shine through the Foggy Dew.

THE HILLS OF KERRY

```
CHORUS:
D
The palm trees wave on high
Em        A    D
Along the fertile shore

Adieu the Hills of Kerry
            G    A
I ne'er will see no more.
     D
Oh why did I leave my home,
Em         A          D
Oh why did I cross the sea,

And leave the small birds singing
        A      D
Around you sweet Tralee.
```

The noble and the brave
Have departed from our shore
They've gone off to a foreign land
Where the wild canyons roar.
No more they'll see the shamrock,
The plant so dear to me,
Or hear the small birds singing
Around sweet Tralee.
REPEAT CHORUS

No more the sun will shine
On that blessed harvest morn
Or hear our reaper singing
In a golden field of corn
There's a balm for every woe
And a cure for every pain,
But the happiness of my darling girl
I will never see again.
REPEAT CHORUS

THE WEARING OF THE GREEN

G
Oh! Paddy dear and did you hear
D
The news that's going round
C   G
The Shamrock is forbid by law
D   G
To grow on Irish ground.

No more St. Patrick's day we'll keep,
D
His colours can't be seen,
C   G
For there's a cruel law against
D   G
The wearing of the green.

I met with Napper Tandy,
And he took me by the hand,
And he said 'How's poor old Ireland
And how does she stand?'
She's the most distressful country
That ever yet was seen,
For they're hangin' men and women
For the wearing of the green.

And if the colour we must wear
Is England's cruel Red,
Let it remind us of the blood
That Ireland has shed.
Then pull the shamrock from your hat
And throw it on the sod,
And never fear, 'twill take root there,
Tho' under foot 'tis trod.
When the law can stop the blades of grass
From growing as they grow,
And when the leaves in summer time
Their colour dare not show,
Then I will change the colour, too,
I wear in my caubeen,
But till that day, please God,
I'll stick to wearing of the Green.

MATT HYLAND

G   C   G
There was a lord who lived in the town,
C   G   D   G
Who had a lovely handsome daughter.
                  C   G
She was courted by a fair young man,
C   G   D G
Who was a servant to her father.
                        D
But when the parents came to know,
    G   C   D G
They swore they'd ban him from the Isle-land,
                      C   G
But the maid she knew that her heart would break
C   G   D G
Had she to part with young Matt Hyland.

So straight away to her love she goes,
Into his room to awake him.
Saying 'arise my love and go away,
This very night you will be taken.
I over-heard my parents say,
In spite of me they will transport you,
So arise my love and go away,
I wish to God I'd gone before you.'

They both sat down upon the bed,
Just for the side of one half hour
And not a word by either said,
As down their cheeks the tears did shower.
She laid her hand upon his breast,
Around his neck her arms entwined,
Not a duke, nor lord, nor an earl I'll wed,
I'll wait for you my own Matt Hyland.

The lord discoursed with his daughter fair,
One night alone in her chamber.
Saying 'we'll give you leave for to bring him back,
Since there's no one can win your favour.'
She wrote a letter then in haste,
Her heart for him was still repining,
They brought him back, to the church they went,
And made a lord of young Matt Hyland.

Road Bowling, South Armagh, 1933

WORKING MAN

CHORUS:

G   C   G
It's a working man I am, and I've been down underground

                            D
And I swear to God if I ever see the sun.

G   C   G
Or for any length of time, I can hold it in my mind,

              D   G
I never again will go down underground.

At the age of sixteen years, I quarrelled with the spears,
Who swore that never be another one
In the dark recess of the mines, where you age before your time
And the coal dust lies heavy on your lungs.
REPEAT CHORUS

At the age of sixty-four, he'll greet you at the door
And gently lead you by the arm,
To the dark recess of the mine, he'll take you back in time,
And tell you of the hardships that were had.
REPEAT CHORUS

The Donohues, (Tinsmiths), Plying their trade at Creegh, Co. Clare, 1944

THE SPANISH LADY

G
As I went down to Dublin city,
C   G   C   D
At the hour of twelve at night,
G
Who should I see but a Spanish lady,
C   G   C   D
Washing her feet by candlelight.
G
First she washed them, then she dried them
                    D
Over a fire of amber coal,
G
In all my life I ne'er did see
    C   G   C   D
A maid so sweet about the soul

CHORUS:
G   Em
Whack fol the toora, toora, laddy,
C   G   D
Whack fol the toora loora-lay
REPEAT CHORUS

As I came back through Dublin city
At the hour of half past eight
Who should I spy but the Spanish lady
Brushing her hair in the broad daylight.
First she tossed it, then she brushed it,
On her lap was a silver comb
In all my life I ne'er did see
A maid so fair since I did roam.
REPEAT CHORUS

As I went back through Dublin city
As the sun began to set
Who should I spy but the Spanish lady
Catching a moth in a golden net.
When she saw me then she fled me
Lifting her petticoat over her knee
In all my life I ne'er did see
A maid so shy as the Spanish Lady.
REPEAT CHORUS

I've wandered north and I've wandered south
Through Stonybatter and Patrick's Close
Up and around the Gloster Diamond
And back by Napper Tandy's house.
Old age has laid her hand on me
Cold as a fire of ashy coals
In all my life I ne'er did see
A maid so sweet as the Spanish Lady.
REPEAT CHORUS

SWEET CARNLOCH BAY

D
When winter was brawling
                        C
O'er high hills and mountains
          D   G
And dark were the clouds
                    D
O'er the deep rolling sea,

I spied a wee lass
                        C
As the daylight was dawning,
D   G
Asking the road
          D
To sweet Carnloch Bay.

I said, 'My wee lassie,
I canna weel tell ye
The number of miles
Or how far it might be,
But if you'll consent
I'll convoy you a wee bit,
And I'll show you the road
To sweet Carnloch Bay.

You turn to the right and pass
Down by the churchyard
Cross over the river
And down by the sea;
We'll call in Pat Hamill's
And have a wee drop there
Just to help us along
To sweet Carnloch Bay.'

Here's a health to Pat Hamill
Likewise the wee lassie
And to every laddie
That's listening to me
And ne'er turn your back
On a bonnie wee lassie
When she's asking the road
To sweet Carnloch Bay.

NEW YORK GIRLS

G   C
As I went down to Broadway
D   G
One evening last July,
              D
I met a maid she asked my trade,
       G
A sailor lad am I.

CHORUS:
          C   D   G
And away shanty my dear Annie,
     D
O you New York girls
              G
Can't you dance the polka.

To Tiffiney's I took her
I did not mind expense,
I bought her a pair of gold ear-rings
And they cost me 15 cents.
REPEAT CHORUS

She said 'my fine new sailor
Now take me home you may'
But when we reached her cottage door
She this to me did say,
'My flash man he's a Yankee
With hair cut short behind,
He wears a pair of tall sea boots
And he sails in the black bow line.'
REPEAT CHORUS

He's homeward bound this evening
And with me he will stay,
So get a move on sailor boy,
Get cracking on your way.
REPEAT CHORUS

I kissed her hard and proper
Before her flash man came,
Saying 'fare thee well me bowery girl
I know your little game.'
REPEAT CHORUS

I wrapped me glad rags round me
And to the docks did steer,
I'll never court another girl,
I'll stick to rum and beer.
REPEAT CHORUS

I joined a Yankee blood boat
And sailed away next morn,
Don't mess around with women lads
You're safer round Cape Horn.
REPEAT CHORUS

THE BONNY BOY

G
The trees are growing tall my love,

The grass is growing green,

And many's the cruel and bitter night
           C D
That I alone have been,
G   C
It is a cruel and bitter night

That I must lie alone,
              G
Oh, the bonny boy is young,

But he's growing.

Oh father dearest father,
I think you did me wrong,
For to go and get me married
To one who is so young
For he is only sixteen years
And I am twenty-one,
But the bonny boy is young,
Though he's growing.

Oh daughter dearest daughter,
I did not do you wrong,
For to go and get you married
To one who is so young,
He will be a match for you
When I'm dead and gone,
Oh the bonny boy is young
But he's growing.

Oh father dearest father,
I'll tell you what I'll do,
I'll send my love to college
For another year or two,
And all around his college cap
I'll bind a ribbon blue,
For to show the other girls
That he's married.

At the early age of sixteen years
He was a married man,
And at the age of seventeen
The father of a son.
But at the age of eighteen o'er his grave
The grass grew green,
Cruel death put an end to his growing.

I'll make my love a shroud
Of the finest Holland brown,
And whilst I am a-weaving it
The tears they will run down,
For once I had a true-love
But now he's lying low,
And I'll nurse his bonny boy
While he's growing.

WHEN YOU WERE SWEET SIXTEEN

G
When first I saw

                 C
The love-light in your eye

D
I dreamt the world

               G
Held naught but joy for me.

And even though

        C
We drifted far apart,

A
I never dream,

            D
But what I dream of thee.

CHORUS:
G
I love you as

      C
I never loved before,

Am   D
Since first I met you

      G
On the village green.

Come to me

           C
Or my dream of love is o'er,

     G
I love you as I loved you,

C   G
When you were sweet,

       D   G
When you were sweet sixteen.

Last night I dreamt
I held your hand in mine,
And once again
You were my happy bride.
I kissed you as I did
In Auld Lang Syne,
As to the church
We wandered side by side.
(*Repeat Chorus Twice*)

Walking Home from School, Carrick, Co. Donegal, 1946

THE OULD ORANGE FLUTE

D   A   D
In the County Tyrone near the town of Dungannon,
                     A
Where mony a ruction myself had a han' in,
D   G   D
Bob Williamson lived, a weaver to trade,
           A   D
And each of us thought him a stout Orange blade.
D   G
On the twelfth of July, as it yearly did come,
D   A
Bob played on the flute, and we banged on the drum;
D   G   D
Ye may talk of your harp, yer piano, or lute,
               A   D
But there's nothing can sound like the ould Orange flute.

CHORUS:
D   G   D
Toor-a-loo, toor-a-lay,
           A   D
Singing toor-al-i-toor-al-i-toor-al-i-ay.

But this treacherous scoundrel, he took us all in,
For he married a Papish named Bridget McGinn,
Turned Popish himself and forsook the oul' cause,
That gave us our freedom, religion and laws.
The boys in the townland made some noise upon it,
And Bob had to fly to the Province of Connaught;
He fled with his wife, and his fixings to boot,
And along with all others the ould Orange flute.
REPEAT CHORUS

At Mass every Sunday to atone for his past deeds,
He said Paters and Aves and counted his beads,
Till after some time, at the priest's own desire,
He went with his ould flute to play in the choir.
He went with his ould flute to play in the Mass,
And the instrument shivered and sighed, 'Oh, alas!'
As he blew it and fingered it made a strange noise,
For the flute would play only 'The Protestant Boys'.
REPEAT CHORUS

Bob started and jumped and he got in a splutter,
And he threw his ould flute in the blessed holy water,
For he thought that this charm would bring some other
sound,
When he played it again, it played 'Croppies Lie Down';
And all he could whistle and finger and blow,
To play Popish music, he found it no go;
'Kick the Pope' and 'Boyne Water' and such like 'twould
sound,
But one Popish squaek in it could not be found.
REPEAT CHORUS

I NEVER WILL MARRY

D   A
I never will marry,
          D   G
I'll be no man's wife,
                  D
I intend to stay single,
A   D
For the rest of my life.

One day as I rambled
Down by the sea shore,
The wind it did whistle
And the waters did roar.

I heard a poor maiden
Make a pitiful cry,
She sounded so lonesome
At the waters nearby.

I never will marry,
I'll be no man's wife,
I intend to stay single,
For the rest of my life.

The shells in the ocean
Will be my deathbed,
And the fish in the water
Swim over my head.

My love's gone and left me,
He's the one I adore,
I never will see him,
No never, no more.

She plunged her fair body
In the water so deep,
She closed her pretty blue
eyes
In the water to sleep.

I never will marry,
I'll be no man's wife,
I intend to stay single,
For the rest of my life.

NANCY SPAIN

G
Of all the stars

That ever shone,
C
Not one does twinkle
G   D
Like your pale blue eyes,

Like golden corn
                G
At harvest time your hair,

Sailing in my boat
C   G   D
The wind gently blows and fills my sail.
                              G
Your sweet scented breath is everywhere

Daylight peeping
Through the curtains of
The passing night time
Is your smile.
The sun in the sky
Is like your laugh.
Come back to me Nancy
Linger for just a little while
Since you left these shores
I know no peace nor joy.

CHORUS:
G   C
No matter where I wander
        G   D
I'm still haunted by your name,
Am   D
The portrait of your beauty
        G
Stays the same.
              C
Standing by the ocean,

Wondering where you've gone,
G   D
If you'll return again,

Where is the ring
          G
I gave to Nancy Spain?

On the day in spring when the snow
Starts to melt and streams to flow,
With the birds I'll sing to you a song.
In the while I'll wander
Down by bluebell grove
Where wild flowers grow
And I'll hope that
Lovely Nancy will return.

DO YOU WANT YOUR OLD LOBBY WASHED DOWN?

G   C
I've a nice little cot and a small bit of land
   D   G
And a place by the side of the sea.
                          C
And I care about no one because I believe
        D   G
There's nobody cares about me.
D   C   G
My peace is destroyed and I'm fairly annoyed
     A   D
By a lassie who works in the town.
G   C
She sighs ev'ry day as she passes the way;
     D   G
Do you want your old lobby washed down?

CHORUS:
Do you want your old lobby washed down,
Con Shine,
Do you want your old lobby washed down?
She sighs ev'ry day as she passes the way;
Do you want your old lobby washed down?

The other day the old landlord came by for his
rent
I told him no money I had,
Besides 'twasn't fair to ask me to pay,
The times were so awfully bad.
He felt discontent at not getting his rent,
And he shook his big head in a frown,
Says he 'I'll take half'. 'But', says I with a laugh
'Do you want your old lobby washed down?'
REPEAT CHORUS

Now the boys look so bashful when they go out
courtin'
They seem to look so very shy,
As to kiss a young maid, sure they seem half
afraid,
But they would if they could on the sly.
But me I do things in a different way,
I don't give a nod or a frown.
When I goes to court I says 'Here goes for
sport,
Do you want your old lobby washed down?'
REPEAT CHORUS

DICEY REILLY

CHORUS:

G   D   G
Ah poor old Dicey Reilly she has taken to the sup,
D   G
And poor old Dicey Reilly she will never give it up,

It's off each morning to the pop,
      D
And then she's in for another little drop,
      G   D G
Ah, the heart of the rowl is Dicey Reilly.

She walks down Fitzgibbon Street with an independent air,
And then it's down to Summerhill, at her the people stare,
She says 'It's nearly half past one,
So I'll nip in for another little one'
Ah, the heart of the rowl is Dicey Reilly.

She owns a little sweetshop at the corner of the street,
And every evening after school I go to wash her feet,
She leaves me there to mind the shop,
While she nips in for another little drop,
Ah, the heart of the rowl is Dicey Reilly.

Burst Water-main, Summer Hill, Dublin City, 1933

24

THE WATER IS WIDE

```
G              C            G              Em          D
The water is wide, I can't cross over, and neither have I wings to fly,
       G                    Em              G
Give me a boat that can carry two, and we shall oar, my love and I.
```

For love is gentle, and love is kind, the sweetest flower when first it's new,
But love grows old and wax is cold, and fades away like morning dew.

There is a ship and she sails the sea, she's loaded deep as deep can be,
But not as deep as the love I'm in I know not how I sink or swim.

Sunday at the seaside, Tramore, Co. Waterford, 1933

THE REAL OLD MOUNTAIN DEW

D
Let grasses grow and waters flow,
       G
In a free and easy way.
   D   G
But give me enough of the rare old stuff
    D   A   D
That's made near Galway Bay.

The gaugers all from Donegal,
From Sligo and Leitrim, too,
Oh, we'll give them the slip and we'll take a sip
Of the real old Mountain Dew.

CHORUS:
Hi the dithery al the dal,
Dal the dal the dithery al,
Al the dal dal dithery al dee,
Hi the dithery al the dal,
Dal the dal the dithery al,
Dal the dal dal dithery al the dee.

At the foot of the hill there's a neat little still
Where the smoke curls up to the sky;
By a whiff of the smell you can plainly tell
That there's poitin, boys, close by.
REPEAT CHORUS

For it fills the air with a perfume rare,
And betwixt both me and you,
As home we roll, we can drink a bowl,
Or a bucketful of mountain dew.
REPEAT CHORUS

Now learned men who use the pen,
Have wrote the praises high
Of the sweet poitin from Ireland green
Distilled from wheat and rye.
REPEAT CHORUS

Away with pills, it will cure all ills,
Of the Pagan, Christian or Jew;
So take off your coat and grease your throat
With the real old mountain dew.
REPEAT CHORUS

JAMES CONNOLLY

D
A great crowd had gathered

Outside of Kilmainham
          G   D
With their heads all uncovered,
      A
They knelt on the ground.
         D
For inside that grim prison

Lay a true Irish soldier,
G   D
His life for his country
A   D
About to lay down.

He went to his death
Like a true son of Ireland,
The firing party
He bravely did face.
Then the order rang out
'Present arms, Fire!'
James Connolly fell
Into a ready made grave.

The black flag they hoisted,
The cruel deed was over,
Gone was the man
Who loved Ireland so well.
There was many a sad heart
In Dublin that morning
When they murdered James
Connolly,
The Irish rebel.

Many years have rolled by
Since the Irish Rebellion,
When the guns of Britannia
They loudly did speak.
And the bold IRA they stood
Shoulder to shoulder,
And the blood from their bodies
Flowed down Sackville Street.

The Four Courts of Dublin,
The English bombarded,
The spirit of freedom,
They tried hard to quell.
But above all the din came the cry
'No Surrender',
'Twas the voice of James Connolly,
The Irish rebel.

SAM HALL

D   G   D   A
Oh, my name it is Sam Hall, chimney sweep, chimney sweep,
     D   G   D
Oh, my name it is Sam Hall, chimney sweep.
     G   D   A
Oh, my name it is Sam Hall and I've robbed both rich and small,
         D   G   D   A
And my neck will pay for all, when I die, when I die,
         D   G   D
And my neck will pay for all, when I die.

Oh, they took me to Coote Hill, in a cart, in a cart,
Oh, they took me to Coote Hill in a cart,
Oh, they took me to Coote Hill and 'twas there I made my will,
For the best of friends must part, so must I, so must I,
For the best of friends must part, so must I.

Up the ladder I did grope, that's no joke, that's no joke,
Up the ladder I did grope, that's no joke,
Up the ladder I did grope and the hangman pulled the rope,
And ne'er a word I spoke, tumbling down, tumbling down,
And ne'er a word I spoke, tumbling down.

SULLIVAN'S JOHN

CHORUS:
D   A   D   C   D   G   D
O'Sullivan's John, to the road you've gone, far away from your native home.
               C   Am   D   C   D
You've gone with the tinker's daughter for along the road to roam.
          C   Am ·   D   C   A
O'Sullivan's John you won't stick it long 'till your belly will soon get slack,
  D   A   D   C   D   G   D
Up along the old road, with a mighty load, and your tool box on your back.

I met Katy Caffey and her neat baby behind on her back strapped on,
She had an oul ash plant in her hand to drive the oul donkey along.
Enquiring in every farmhouse, as along the road she passed,
Oh where would she get an old pot to mend, and where would she get an ass.

There's a hairy ass fair in the County Clare, in a place they call Spancel Hill,
Where my brother James got a rap of a hames, and poor Paddy they tried to kill.
They loaded him up in an oul ass and cart, as along the road to go,
Oh bad luck to the day that he roved away for to join with the tinker band.
Repeat Chorus

Policeman and Child, Cowper Gardens Rathmines, Dublin, 1942

BIG STRONG MAN (SYLVEST)

D   A
Have you heard about the big strong man, he lived in a caravan.

                                         D
Have you heard about the Jeffrey Johnston fight, oh what a hell of a fight.

                                     A
You can take all the heavy-weights you got, we gotta lad who will beat the whole lot,

                                   D
He used to ring the bells in the belfry, now he's gonna fight Jack Dempsey.

                                    A
Was me brother Sylvest what's he got (spoken) a row of forty medals on his chest, big chest

                                   D
He killed fifty bad men in the West, he knew no rest.

Think of the man's hell fire, don't push just shove,

Plenty of room for you and me, got an arm like a leg,

                          A
And a punch that would sink a battleship, big ship,

                                  D
Takes all the army and the navy to put the wind up Sylvest.

He thought he'd take a trip to Italy, he thought that he'd go by sea,
He dived off the harbour in New York, he swam like a great big shark.
He saw the Lusitania in distress, put the Lusitania on his chest,
Drank all the water in the sea, he walked all the way to Italy.
REPEAT CHORUS

He thought he'd take a trip to old Japan, they brought out the big brass band,
He played every instrument they'd got, what a lad, he played the whole lot.
The old church bell will ring, the old church choir will sing,
They all turned out to say farewell, to my big brother Sylvest.
REPEAT CHORUS

SALLY BROWN

G   D   G
Shipped on board a Liverpool liner, Wae Hae, roll on board,

                  C   G   D   G   D   G
And we rolled all night and we rolled all day, I will spend my money on Sally Brown.

Miss Sally Brown she's a nice young lady, Wae Hae, roll on board,
Oh we rolled all night rolled till the day, Gonna spend my money on Sally Brown.

Her mammy doesn't like a tarry sailor, Wae Hae, roll on board,
Oh we rolled all night rolled till the day, Gonna spend my money on Sally Brown.

She wants her to marry a one legged Captain, Wae Hae, roll on board,
Oh we rolled all night rolled till the day, Gonna spend my money on Sally Brown.

WHISKEY IN THE JAR

G
As I was going over,

Em
The Kilmagenny mountain,

C
I met with Captain Farrell

G
And his money he was counting,

I first produced my pistol,

Em
And then I drew my sabre,

C
Saying 'Stand and deliver

G
For I am a bold deceiver.'

CHORUS

D
With me ring dum a doodle um dah,

G
Whack fol the daddy o,

C
Whack fol the daddy o,

G   D   G
There's whiskey in the jar.

He counted out his money
And it made a pretty penny,
I put it in my pocket
And I gave it to my Jenny.
She sighed and she swore
That she never would betray me
But the devil take the women
For they never can be easy
REPEAT CHORUS

I went into my chamber
All for to take a slumber
I dreamt of gold and jewels
And for sure it was no wonder
But Jenny drew my charges
And she filled them up with water
And she sent for Captain Farrell
To be ready for the slaughter
REPEAT CHORUS

And 'twas early in the morning
Before I rose to travel
Up comes a band of footmen
And likewise Captain Farrell;
I then produced my pistol,
For she stole my sabre,
But I couldn't shoot the water,
So a prisoner I was taken.
REPEAT CHORUS

And if anyone can aid me,
Its my brother in the army
If I could learn his station
In Cork or in Killarney,
And if he'd come and join me,
We'd go roving in Kilkenny
I'll engage he'll treat me fairer
Than my darling sporting Jenny.
REPEAT CHORUS

DINGLE BAY

D   G   D
The sun was sinking o'er the westward,

Em
The fleet is leaving Dingle shore,

D   G   D
I watch the men row in their currachs,

G   A
As they mark the fishing grounds

D
Near Sceilig Mór.

G   D
All thro' the night men toil until the daybreak,

While at home their wives

Em
And sweethearts kneel and pray,

D   G   D
That God might guard them and protect them,

G   A   D
And bring them safely back to Dingle Bay.

I see the green Isle of Valentia
I mind the days around Lough Lein
The gannets swinging with abandon
As they watch the silver store
That comes their way.
I also see a ship on the horizon,
She is sailing to a country far away,
On board are exiles feeling lonely,
As they wave a fond farewell to Dingle Bay.

Now years have passed
Since I came homeward
And time has left me old and grey.
I sit and muse about my childhood
And the happy times
I spent near Dingle Bay.
I see again the green isle of Valentia,
And the Isle of Innishmore seems far away,
And I'm always dreaming
About my childhood
And the happy times I spent near Dingle Bay.

THREE SCORE AND TEN

CHORUS:

D
And it's three score and ten

Boys and men were lost from

Grimsby Town,

     A   D
From Yarmouth down to Scarborough

                 A
Many hundreds more were drowned.

  D
Their fishing boats, their herring,

Their fishing smacks as well;

 A
They went to fight the bitter night

          D
And battle with the swell.

Me thinks I see a host of craft
Spreading their sails a-lea,
As down the Humber they did lie,
Bound for the cold North Sea.
Me thinks I see's a wee small craft,
And crew with hearts so brave,
They went to earn their daily bread,
Upon the restless waves.
REPEAT CHORUS

October night brought such a sight,
'Twas never seen before,
There were masts and yards of broken
spars
Washed-up on the shore,
There was many a heart of sorrow,
There was many a heart so brave,
There was many a true and noble lad
To find a watery grave.

THE MERRY PLOUGHBOY

D   A
Oh I am a merry ploughboy,

      G   D
And I plough the fields all day,

         A
Till a sudden thought came to my mind,

           D
That I should run away.

           G   D A
Well I'm sick and tired of slavery,

    G   D
Since the day that I was born,

    A
So I'm off to join the IRA,

           D
And I'm off tomorrow morn.

CHORUS:

D   A
Well I'm off to Dublin in the green, in the green,

        G   D
Where the helmets glisten in the sun.

        A
Where the bayonets flash, and the rifles clash

             D
To the echo of a Thompson gun.

I'll leave aside my pick and spade,
And I'll leave aside my plough,
I'll leave aside my old grey mare,
For no more I'll need them now.
And I'll leave aside my Mary,
She's the girl that I adore,
Well I wonder if she'll think of me,
When she hears the cannons roar.
REPEAT CHORUS

And when this war is over,
And dear old Ireland's free,
I'll take her to the church to wed,
And a rebel's wife she'll be.
REPEAT CHORUS

THE RARE OUL' TIMES

```
G                    C   G              C
Based on songs and stories, heroes of renown,
G                              D
Are the passing tales and glories, that once was Dublin town
G                    C   G                         C
The hallowed halls and houses, the haunting children's rhymes,
G              C          D       G
That once was part of Dublin, in the rare old times.
```

CHORUS:

```
            C G                  Em
Ring-a-ring-a-Rosie, as the light declines,
  G          C        D         G
I remember Dublin city, in the rare oul' times.
```

My name it is Sean Dempsey, as Dublin as can be,
Born hard and late in Pimlico, in a house that ceased to be.
By trade I was a cooper, lost out to redundancy.
Like my house that fell to progress, my trade's a memory.
And I courted Peggy Dignan, as pretty as you please,
A rogue and child of Mary, from the rebel Liberties.
I lost her to a student chap, with skin as black as coal.
When he took her off to Birmingham, she took away my soul.
REPEAT CHORUS

The years have made me bitter, the gargle dims my brain,
'Cause Dublin keeps on changing, and nothing seems the same.
The Pillar and the Met. have gone, the Royal long since pulled down,
As the great unyielding concrete, makes a city of my town.
REPEAT CHORUS

Fare thee well, sweet Anna Liffey, I can no longer stay,
And watch the new glass cages, that spring up along the Quay.
My mind's too full of memories, too old to hear new chimes,
I'm part of what was Dublin, in the rare ould times.
REPEAT CHORUS

The Ice Cream Man, Stillorgan, Co. Dublin, 1939

THE STAR OF THE COUNTY DOWN

Em   G   D
Near to Banbridge town, in the county Down,

  Em   G
One morning in July

    Em   G   D
Down a boreen green came a sweet colleen

      Em
And she smiled as she passed me by;

  G   D
Oh she looked so neat from her two white feet

    Em   G
To the sheen of her nut-brown hair,

      Em   G   D
Sure the coaxing elf, I'd to shake myself,

      Em
To make sure I was standing there.

CHORUS:

      G   D
Oh from Bantry Bay up to Derry Quay,

      Em   G
And from Galway to Dublin town,

    Em   G   D
No maid I've seen like the sweet colleen

    Em
That I met in County Down.

As she onward sped I shook my head
And I gazed with a feeling quare,
'And I said', says I to a passer-by
'Who's the maid with the nut-brown hair?'
Oh he smiled at me, and with pride says he:
'That's the gem of Ireland's crown,
She's young Rosie McCann,
from the banks of the Bann,
She's the star of the County Down'.
REPEAT CHORUS

She'd a soft brown eye and a look so sly
And a smile like the rose in June,
And you hung on each note from her lily-white
throat,
As she lilted an Irish tune.
At the pattern dance you were held in trance
As she tripped through a reel or a jig,
And when her eyes she'd roll, she'd coax upon
my soul
A spud from a hungry pig.
REPEAT CHORUS

I've travelled a bit, but never was hit,
Since my roving career began;
But fair and square I surrendered thee
To the charm of young Rosie McCann
With a heart to let and no tenant yet,
Did I meet within shawl or gown.
But in she went and I asked no rent
From the star of the County Down.
REPEAT CHORUS

At the crossroads fair I'll be surely there
And I'll dress in my Sunday clothes,
And I'll try sheep's eyes and deludhering lies
On the heart of the nut-brown Rose.
No pipe I smoke, no horse I'll yoke
Though my plough with rust turns brown
Till a smiling bride by my own fireside
Sits the star of the County Down.
REPEAT CHORUS

THE ZOOLOGICAL GARDENS

D   C   A
Ah, thunder and lightning is no lark,

      D   A
When Dublin city is in the dark.

      D
If you've any money go up to the Park

                    A   D
And view the Zoological Gardens.

Last Sunday night we had no dough
So I took the mot up to see the Zoo,
We saw the lions and the kangaroos
Inside the Zoological Gardens.

Well we went out there by Castleknock
Said the mot to me 'Sure we court by the Lough'
Then I knew she was one of the rare old stock,
Inside the Zoological Gardens.

Said the mot to me 'My dear friend Jack,
Sure, I'd like a ride on the elephant's back.'
'If you don't get out of that I'll give you such a
crack
Inside the Zoological Gardens.'

We went out there on our honeymoon,
Said the mot to me 'If you don't come soon,
I'll have to sleep with the hairy baboon,
Inside the Zoological Gardens.'

REILLY'S DAUGHTER

```
G                                      C
As I was sitting by the fire, talking to old Reilly's daughter,
G                                                    C
Suddenly a thought came into my head; I'd like to marry old Reilly's daughter.
```

CHORUS:
```
G                                 C        G
Giddy I Ay, Giddy I Ay, Giddy I Ay, for the one-eyed Reilly.
```

Giddy I Ay, bang, bang, bang, play it on your big brass drum.

For Reilly played on the big brass drum, Reilly had a mind for murder and slaughter
Reilly had a bright red glittering eye, and he kept that eye on his lovely daughter.
REPEAT CHORUS

Her hair was black and her eyes were blue the colonel and the major and the captain sought her
The sergeant and the private and the drummer boy, too, but they never had a chance with
O'Reilly's daughter.
REPEAT CHORUS

I got me a ring and a parson too, I got me a 'scratch' in the married quarter
Settled me down to a peaceful life, as happy as a king with O'Reilly's daughter.
REPEAT CHORUS

Suddenly a footstep on the stair, who should it be but the one-eyed Reilly
With two pistols in his hand looking for the man who married his daughter.
REPEAT CHORUS

I took O'Reilly by the hair, rammed his head in a pail of water,
Fired his pistols in the air, a darned sight quicker than I married his daughter.
REPEAT CHORUS

THE MINSTREL BOY

```
G        C      G              C      G      D   G
The minstrel boy to the war is gone, in the ranks of death you'll find him;
                         C      G            D   G
His father's sword he has girded on, and his wild harp slung behind him;
   D C        D                     C      G      C D G
'Land of song,' said the warrior bard, though all the world betrays thee,
         C      G              C   G        D      G
One sword at least thy rights shall guard, one faithful harp shall praise thee.'
```

The Minstrel fell! but the foeman's chain could not bring that proud soul under;
The harp he loved ne'er spoke again, for he tore its chords asunder;
And said, 'No chains shall sully thee, thou soul of love and bravery!
Thy songs were made for the pure and free, they shall never sound in slavery.'

THE LARK IN
THE MORNING

G
The lark in the morning
D
She rises off her nest,
Em
And she goes off in the air

With the dew all on her breast

And like the jolly ploughboy
D
She whistles and she sings,
Em
She goes home in the evening

With the dew all on her wings.

Oh, Roger the ploughboy
He is a dashing blade,
He goes whistling and singing
For yonder leafy shade.
He met with dark-eyed Susan,
She's handsome I declare,
And she is far mor enticing
Than the birds all in the air.

As they were coming home
From the rakes of the town,
The meadow bein' all mown
And the grass had been cut down.
As they should chance to tumble
All on the new-mown hay,
Oh, it's kiss me now or never,
This bonnie lass would say.

When twenty long weeks
Were over and past,
Her mammy asked the reason
Why she thickened round the waist.
'It was the pretty ploughboy,'
This girl then did say,
For he asked me for to tumble
All on the new-mown hay.

Here's a health to you ploughboys
Wherever you may be,
That like to have a bonnie lass
A-sittin' on each knee.
With a pint of good strong porter
He'll whistle and he'll sing,
And the ploughboy is as happy
As a prince or a king.

ST. PATRICK WAS
A GENTLEMAN

Em
Saint Patrick was a gentleman,
      D
He came of decent people,
         Em
In Dublin town he built a church,
      G   D   G
And on it put a steeple.
Em   C
His father was a Callaghan,
      G   D
His mother was a Brady,
   Em   C
His aunt was an O'Shaughnessy,
      G   D
And his uncle was a Grady.

CHORUS:
              Em
Then success to bold St. Patrick's fist,
   G   D
He was a saint so clever,
          Em
He gave the snakes an awful twist
      G   D   G
And banished them forever.

There's not a mile in Ireland's isle
Where the dirty vermin musters,
Where'er he put his dear forefoot
He murder'd them in clusters.
The toads went hop, the frogs went plop,
Slap dash into the water,
And the beasts committed suicide
To save themselves from slaughter.

Nine hundred thousand vipers blue
He charmed with sweet discourses,
And dined on them at Killaloo
In soups and second courses.
When blind worms crawling on the grass
Disgusted all the nation,
He gave them a rise and open'd their eyes
To a sense of their situation.

The Wicklow hills are very high,
And so's the hill of Howth, sir,
But there's a hill much higher still,
Ay, higher than them both, sir.
'Twas on the top of this high hill
St. Patrick preached the 'sarmint',
He drove the frogs into the bogs,
And bothered all the 'varmint'.

HOME BOYS HOME

D
Oh when I was just a young boy,

Sure I longed to see the world,

  A
To sail across the sea in ships

      D
And see the sails unfurled.

         G
I went to seek my fortune

    D   A
On the far side of the hill,

I've wandered far and wide,

              D
And of travel I've had my fill.

CHORUS:
D
And it's home, boys, home,

Home I'd like to be,

G   D
Home for a while

        A
In the old country,

     D   G
Where the oak and the ash

     D   A
And the bonny rowan tree,

Are all growin' greener

       D
In the old country.

Well I left my love behind me
And I sailed across the tide,
I said that I'd be back again
And take her for my bride,
But many years have passed and gone,
And still I'm far away,
I know she is a fond true-love
And waiting for the day.
REPEAT CHORUS

Now I've learned there's more to life
Than to wander and to roam,
Happiness and peace of mind
Can best bc found at home.
For money can't buy happiness
And money cannot bind,
So I'm going back tomorrow
To the girl I left behind.
REPEAT CHORUS

FAR AWAY
IN AUSTRALIA

G   C   G
Sweetheart I'm bidding you fond farewell,
             C   D
Murmured a youth one day
C   D   C   G
I'm off to a new land my fortune to try
                 D   G
And I'm ready to sail away.
G   Em   Am   D
Far away in Australia
Em   Am   C
Soon will faith be kind,
              Am   G
And I will be ready to welcome the lass,
        D   G
The girl I left behind.

Must we be parted his fair one cried,
I cannot let you go,
Still I must leave you the young man replied,
But only for a while you know,
Far away in Australia
Soon will faith be kind,
And I will be ready to welcome the lass,
The girl I left behind.

Whether in success or failure,
I will always be true,
Proudly each day in the land far away,
I'll be building a home for you.
Far away in Australia
Soon will faith be kind,
And I will be ready to welcome the lass,
The girl I left behind.

Daily she waits at the old cottage gates,
Watching the whole day through,
Till a sweet message comes over the waves,
In the new world are joined the two,
Far away in Australia
Soon will faith be kind,
And I will be ready to welcome the lass,
The girl I left behind.

THE ENNISKILLEN DRAGOON

D   A
Fare thee well Enniskillen,
D
Fare thee well for a while,
   A
To all your fair waters
    D
And every green isle,

Oh your green isle will flourish,
  A   D
Your fair waters flow,

While I from old Ireland
  A   D
An exile must go.

They were all dressed out
Like gentlemen's sons,
With their bright shining swords
And carbine guns,
With their silver mounted pistols,
She observed them full soon,
Because that she loved
Her Enniskillen Dragoon.

The bright sons of Mars,
As they stood on the right,
Their armour did shine
Like the bright stars at night,
Says she, 'lovely Willie,
You've listed too soon,
To serve as a Royal
Enniskillen Dragoon.'

O beautiful Flora,
Your pardon I crave,
Until now and forever
I will be your slave,
Your parents insult you
Both morning and noon,
For fear you should wed
Your Enniskillen Dragoon.

O now, dearest Willie,
Mind what you say,
For children are obliged
Their parents to obey,
But when you're leaving Ireland,
They all change their tune,
Saying, the Lord be with you,
Enniskillen Dragoon.

Farewell Enniskillen,
Farewell for a while,
And all around the borders
Of Erin's Isle,
And when the wars are over,
You'll return in full bloom,
They'll all welcome home
The Enniskillen Dragoon.

Now the war is over,
And they have returned at last,
The regiment lies in Dublin,
And Willie's got a pass,
Last Sunday they were married,
And Willie was the groom,
And now she enjoys
Her Enniskillen Dragoon.

RODDY MCCORLEY

D
See the host of fleet foot men
    G   D
Who sped with faces wan,
              G   D
From farmstead and from fishers cot,
        G   A
Along the banks of Bann.
     D   G   D
They come with vengeance in their eyes,
        G   A
Too late, too late are they,
        D
For young Roddy McCorley goes to die
      G   D
On the bridge of Toome today.

When he last stepped up that street,
His shining pike in hand,
Behind him marched in grim array,
A stalwart earnest band,
For Antrim town, for Antrim town,
He led them to the fray,
And young Roddy McCorley goes to die
On the bridge of Toome today.

Up the narrow streets he steps,
Smiling proud and young,
About the hemp rope on his neck,
The golden ringlets clung.
There was never a tear in his blue eyes,
Both sad and bright are they,
For young Roddy McCorley goes to die
On the bridge of Toome today.

THE GOOD SHIP KANGAROO

```
A            G                          D
At first I was a waiting man that lived at home at ease
             G                A         D
But now I am a mariner that ploughs the angry seas
```

I always loved seafarin' life I bid my love adieu
I shipped as steward and cook, me boys, on board the Kangaroo.

CHORUS:
Oh I never thought she would prove false or either prove untrue
As we sailed away through Milford Bay on board the Kangaroo.

'Oh think of me, oh think of me', she mournfully did say
'When you are in a foreign land and I am far away.
Now take this lucky trupenny bit, it'll make you bear in mind,
That lovin' trustin' faithful heart you left in tears behind.'
REPEAT CHORUS

'Cheer up, cheer up, my own true love. Don't weep so bitterly.'
She sobbed, she sighed, she choked, she cried and could not say goodbye.
'I won't be gone for very long, 'tis but a month or two.
When I will return again of course I'll marry you.'
REPEAT CHORUS

Our vessel she was homeward bound from many's the foreign shore
And many's the foreign present unto me love I bore.
I brought tortoises from Tenerife and toys from Timbuktu
A china rat, a Bengal cat and a Bombay cockatoo.
REPEAT CHORUS

Paid off I sought her dwellin' on a street above the town
Where an ancient dame upon the line was hangin' out her gown.
'Where is me love?' She's married, sir, six months ago
To a smart young man who drives the van for Chaplin, Son and Co.
REPEAT CHORUS

Here's a health to dreams of married life, to soap, to suds and blue,
Heart's true love and patent starch and washin' soda too.
I'll go unto some distant shore, no longer can I stay,
And with some China hottentot I'll throw myself away.
REPEAT CHORUS

Me love, she is not a foolish girl, her age it is two score.
Me love, she is not a spinster, she's been married twice before.
I cannot say it was her wealth that stole me heart away,
She's a starcher and a laundress in a laundry for one and nine a day.
REPEAT CHORUS

ALSO AVAILABLE IN THIS SERIES:
Duncles 50 Great Irish Ballads Volume 1
Duncles 50 Great Irish Ballads Volume 2

VOLUME 1	VOLUME 2
SONNY'S DREAM	THE FIELDS OF ATHENRY
GRACE	RAGLAN ROAD
TEDDY O'NEALE	THE GREEN FIELDS OF FRANCE
WILD ROVER, THE	A BUNCH OF THYME
STREETS OF NEW YORK, THE	SONG FOR IRELAND
THE BAND PLAYED 'WALTZING MATHILDA'	THE BLACK VELVET BAND
MY LOVELY ROSE OF CLARE	JAMES CONNOLLY
MARY FROM DUNGLOE	MUIRSHEEN DURKIN
THE LOWLANDS OF HOLLAND	RED IS THE ROSE
EASY AND SLOW	TWENTY-ONE YEARS
DOWN BY THE GLENSIDE	THE WEST'S AWAKE
THE CLIFFS OF DOONEEN	LANIGAN'S BALL
A NATION ONCE AGAIN	JUG OF PUNCH
ARTHUR MC BRIDE	I'LL TELL ME MA
THE GLENDALOUGH SAINT	BOTANY BAY
PADDY LAY BACK	THE BOYS OF FAIR HILL
THE GYPSY	PEGGY GORDON
IN DUBLIN'S FAIR CITY	THE ROSE OF ALLENDALE
THE ROSE OF MOONCOIN	THE BARD OF ARMAGH
THE RISING OF THE MOON	THE GOLDEN JUBILEE
OLD MAID IN THE GARRET	THE TOWN OF BALLYBAY
NOVA SCOTIA	AS I ROVED OUT
. . . . and many others	. . . . and many others

If you have stumbled your way through the chords in this book,
you may like to know that Ossian has also published the following:

Basic Chords for Guitar and How to Use 'Em
144 easy chords in all keys, with sections on tuning, strums, use
of capo and a selection of easy songs.
By John Loesberg (OMB 59)

Instant Guitar Chords
864 chords - 24 chord types for every key, each shown in 3
positions on the neck. Suitable for Folk, Pop, Rock and Jazz.
By John Loesberg (OMB 60)

Chords for Mandolin/Irish Banjo/Bouzouki
Easy chords in all keys.
By John Loesberg (OMB 61)